the TAPAS cookbook

the TAPAS cookbook

seventy delicious recipes

to capture the flavors of Spain

Adrian Linssen with Sara Cleary

NEW
BURLINGTON
BOOKS

A QUINTET BOOK

Published by New Burlington Books
6 Blundell Street, London, N7 9BH

ISBN 1-86155-267-X
Reprinted 1999, 2001, 2002
This book was designed and produced by
Quintet Publishing Limited
6 Blundell Street, London, N7 9BH

CREATIVE DIRECTOR: richard dewing
ART DIRECTOR: lucy parissi
DESIGNERS: simon balley and joanna hill
PROJECT EDITOR: amanda dixon
EDITOR: gail dixon-smith
PHOTOGRAPHER: tim ferguson hill
FOOD STYLIST: alison austin

Picture Credits
Travel Ink: pages 7(b), 8(t)
Life File: pages 6(t), (b), 7(t), 8(b), 9(t)

Special thanks to Ana Henriquez Marteau for her help with the
subtleties of the Spanish language, and for supplying the recipes
for Garlic Potatoes and Russian Salad.

Typeset in Great Britain by
Central Southern Typesetters, Eastbourne
Manufactured in Singapore by
Pica Colour Separation Overseas Pte Ltd
Printed in Singapore by Star Standard Industries (Pte) Ltd
Material in this book previously appeared in *Tapas*
by Adrian Linssen with Sara Cleary

Some recipes in this book use raw eggs. Because of the
slight risk of salmonella, raw eggs should not be
served to the very young, the ill or the elderly, or to
pregnant women.

contents

above: **Hotel bar in Colmenar, Andalusia.**

R ipe with the flavors of history and seasoned with the tastes of modern time, Spanish *tapas* are mouthwatering little dishes of delight.

According to Spanish folklore, the first *tapa* was a slice of cured ham thrown hastily atop a glass of sherry to keep out the flies. The ham was so popular it gave birth to the tradition of Spanish *tapas*—literally "lids" or "covers." Today cured ham, *jamón serrano*, is served alongside dishes from all over Spain; from fresh squid and salted almonds to stewed olives and goat cheese. They present an abundance of tastes, smells, and colors; and invite the uninhibited mixing of each—truly both a gourmand's and a chef's delight!

Tapas bars are at the center of every Spanish community, from the remote, relaxed mountain villages to the busy, crowded city districts. Twice a day, like clockwork, Spaniards congregate at their favorite local bar for a chilled sherry or a glass of white wine, conversation with their friends and, of course, *tapas*.

below: **Orange stall in Javea, Alicante.**

A good *tapas* bar is an Aladdin's cave of indulgence, filled with gastronomic treasures. Arranged along the counter is an assortment of cheeses, shrimp, scallops, garlic, chicken, omelets, and salads. From the ceiling hang cured hams and stacked against the back wall are dusty bottles of wine.

Served as *media ración*, or appetizers, flavorful dishes like Garlic Mushrooms, Fried Squid, or Goat Cheese with Tarragon and Garlic Marinade awaken the palate while leaving room for heartier dishes. Make no mistake, however; *tapas* are not limited in size, ingredients, or to a fixed course in a meal. They are equally delicious eaten as *ración*—with enough for a group to share as bar snacks, or for one hungry bar-goer to eat as a main course.

above. **Fishermen in Nerja, Andalusia.**

below: **Menu of** *raciones,* **Madrid.**

above: **Tiled façade in Alicante province.**

Eating "*tapas*-style" can spice up any occasion. Impress your guests at your next barbecue with some *tapas*-inspired dishes: throw on a few Marinated Lamb Cutlets and Spicy Moorish Kabobs, and serve with Garlic Potatoes and Tomato Salad with Olives.

Add a taste of the sea with Spicy Monkfish Brochettes or Bacon-wrapped Shrimp with Sour Cream. For special festivities get extra tangy with Oysters Bloody Mary—mix an ice-cold Bloody Mary, carefully open the oysters, loosen from the shell, pour in the juice... and swallow!

Even vegetarians can relish in their *tapas*. Many main and side dishes can be tastily prepared without meat: favorites include Roast Potatoes in Sweet Hot Sauce; Three Peppers in

above. **Mosque exterior in Cordoba, Andalusia.**

Tomato & Garlic; Green Beans Tapa; and the national staple, the Spanish Omelet— or *Tortilla*.

The more exotic and more involved tapas are ideal served at special celebrations. Lobster and Chicken Brochettes, Chicken Livers with Sherry Vinegar, and Spanish Style Squid or Chicken Pies—or *Empanadas*—make tantalizingly exotic main dishes. Slice open an *Empanada*, and the wafting aroma is guaranteed to bring smiles of anticipation to the faces of your guests. On a hot day, what better than a colorful chilled Shrimp Salad—or *Ceviche*—to cool you down and spice things up?

Tapas can be served in a shell or on a brochette, with or without a sauce. They can be large or small, hot or cold, complex or simple. The dishes range from vegetable to egg and cheese, fish,

above: **Archway and cobbled street in Frigliana, Andalucia.**

shellfish, and a host of fresh and cured meats. The recipes are adaptable and there is something for everyone and for every occasion. The only difficulty lies in the choosing.

Note: Use a vegetable oil of your choice in recipes where an unspecified oil is called for.

These recipes, unless otherwise indicated, make *tapa* for four. This is intended as a rough guide only as *tapas*, by their very nature, vary in size.

Seafood Tapas

Marisco

Scallops with Lime and Crab

Vieiras con Cangrejo y Lima

12 small to medium, or 6 large scallops (slice the latter across horizontally)
Juice of 4 limes
Juice of 2 oranges
1½ Tbsp brandy
1 small piece of gingerroot, chopped fine
Salt and freshly ground black pepper
1 cup white crab meat

preparation

To pry open the scallops place them dark side of shell down and slip a sharp knife through the hinge to sever the muscle which holds the scallop to the shell.

Trim away the muscular "foot." Wash and place in the refrigerator, in the cleaned shells, on a tray.

Mix the lime juice, orange juice, brandy, ginger, and seasoning together and spoon over the scallops. Marinate for 4 to 6 hours. The scallops will go opaque and be firm to the touch when ready.

Lightly season the crab meat and flake over the scallops.

Serve well chilled.

Scallops in Tomato Sauce

Vieiras en Salsa Tomate

12 small or 6 large scallops
½ stick butter
⅔ cup dry white wine
½ cup shredded Parmesan cheese
Lemon wedges, to serve

For the sauce
½ stick butter
¼ cup flour
2½ cups milk, warmed
½ Tbsp tomato paste
1 tsp garlic, crushed
1 tsp sugar
2 large tomatoes, peeled and chopped fine
1 Tbsp heavy cream
½ cup shredded Parmesan cheese
½ tsp freshly ground black pepper

For the potato
2 lb potatoes
Salt
¾ stick butter
2 egg yolks
2 Tbsp light cream, warmed
Salt and freshly ground black pepper
2 tsp parsley, chopped

to prepare the scallops

Open by placing in the oven at 450°F for a few minutes. Cut out the scallop with a sharp knife, trim off the "foot," and wash well. Wash the shells and keep to one side.

Separate the pink coral from the white of the scallop and keep both in the refrigerator.

to prepare the sauce

Melt the butter, stir in the flour, and cook to a sandy texture. Gradually whisk in the warmed milk, then the tomato paste, garlic, and sugar. Stir occasionally and simmer for 20 minutes to cook the flour. Lower the heat and stir in the chopped tomatoes, cream, cheese, and pepper. Keep to one side until needed.

While the sauce is cooking, prepare the mashed potato. Peel, wash, and chop the potatoes into even pieces, place in salted water, bring to a boil, and cook until soft. Drain thoroughly, return to the pot, cover, and place over a low heat, shaking occasionally to dry them out. Mash with ¼ stick butter. With a wooden spoon, mix in the yolks and the rest of the butter. Beat in the warm cream and season well. Stir in the chopped parsley. Take a piping bag, with a star nozzle, and fill it with the potato.

to cook the scallops

Melt the butter and when hot, add the scallops (keeping back the pink corals, as they take less cooking) and turn to seal both sides. Add the wine, bring to a boil, then add the pink corals and simmer for 3 minutes.

Place the shells on a cookie sheet, and spoon 1 teaspoon of sauce into each shell. Place a scallop and a coral back into each shell. Spoon the sauce over. Pipe the potato in little stars around the edge of the shell. Sprinkle the cheese over and place in a hot oven (425°F) for 5 minutes or until cheese is browned. Serve with lemon wedges.

Fried Squid

Sepia Frita

2 lb squid, cleaned
3 eggs, beaten
Flour
Salt and freshly ground
black pepper
Lemon wedges, to serve

to clean the squid

Cut off the legs just below the eyes and keep to one side. Squeeze the top of the legs and the beak will pop out; discard it. Empty the body sac over the sink, by thrusting the fingers under the plastic-like backbone. Pull out the backbone and discard it. Pull the guts carefully, so that they come out in one piece, and discard. Rinse the inside of the sac. Remove the fins firmly from where they join the body. The purple membranous skin will then easily peel off. Rinse well and slice the body across into ½-inch thick rings. Combine with the legs and rinse again. Place a pot of water on the stove, with enough water to cover the squid. When boiling, add the squid and blanch for 1 minute. Remove and cool immediately under cold water. The squid are now ready for further use.

preparation

Mix the eggs well over the squid, using your hands. Season. Slowly add enough flour, mixing thoroughly to a thick paste. Heat the deep-fryer to 365°F and carefully lower the squid piece by piece, and in batches, into the oil. Shake and fry to a golden color. Remove, drain, season, and serve with lemon wedges.

Marinated Smelt

Chanquetes Fritos

1 lb bag frozen smelt,
defrosted (for about 2
hours at room
temperature)
1 Tbsp parsley, chopped
2 tsp garlic, crushed
Juice of 2 lemons (or enough
to cover the fish while
they marinate)
2 shallots, chopped fine
2 tsp freshly ground
black pepper
½ tsp salt
4 Tbsp olive oil

preparation

Remove heads of smelt. Split lengthwise for the larger
ones, and leave the small ones whole. Pull out the
bone of the larger ones.

Place on a tray or in a square dish (not a metal dish).
Cover with the parsley, garlic, lemon juice, shallots,
and seasoning.

Leave to marinate for 24 hours in the refrigerator.

Drain off the excess juice. Cover with the oil, leave for
one hour, and serve.

Deep-fried Smelt

Chanquetes en Escabeche

1 lb frozen smelt
½ cup milk, at room
temperature
Flour, to coat
Oil, to fry
Salt, preferably sea salt
Lemon wedges, to serve

preparation

Shake the frozen smelt into the milk. If the milk is too
cold, small ice particles will form; if this happens, add a
few drops of hot water.

Shake the smelt thoroughly into the flour. Toss
thoroughly in a sifter to remove excess flour.

Place the fish in a frying basket and fry in hot oil for 3
minutes in 2 or 3 batches; too many together will stick
in the basket. If you do not have a frying basket, pan-
fry in 2 tablespoons of oil until cooked through.

Sprinkle with the salt and serve immediately with
lemon wedges.

Fried Sardines

Sardinas Fritas

12 sardines (about 4-in long)
1/2 cup seasoned flour
Salt and freshly ground
black pepper
Oil, to fry
Lemon wedges, to serve

For the marinade, blend together:
2 tsp parsley, chopped
4 Tbsp lemon juice
1/2 tsp garlic, crushed
Salt and freshly ground
black pepper
1 Tbsp olive oil

Ingredients for the sauce/dip
1 large tomato, skinned and
chopped
1 small green bell pepper,
seeded and chopped
1/2 small onion, chopped
Enough mayonnaise to bind
Salt and freshly ground
black pepper

to prepare the sardines

Take the sardines (if the head is on, leave it) and cut through the bellies lengthwise without cutting through the bone. Butterfly the fish.

Paint the marinade on the fish, and leave to marinate for 20 minutes.

Shake the flour over the fish, dusting until well-covered. Shake off any excess flour. Season.

Heat the oil until hot and fry the sardines, turning to brown both sides.

to prepare the sauce/dip

Mix all the ingredients together, then either spoon onto plates with the sardines, or use as a dip.

Serve with lemon wedges.

Monkfish with Anchovy Sauce

Rape con Salsa de Anchoas

1 lb monkfish, skinned,
cleaned, and cubed
1 Tbsp freshly ground
black pepper
Flour
½ cup olive oil
¼ cup anchovy paste
Parsley, to garnish

preparation

Season the fish and lightly dust with flour.

Heat the oil in a pan, add the fish pieces, and lower
the heat. Cover and cook for 4 to 6 minutes, until the
flesh is still quite springy and very slightly underdone.
Remove from the oil and keep warm.

Add the anchovy paste to the pan and bring to a boil.

Taste for a strong, sharp, peppery flavor.

Return the fish to the pan, stir, and serve garnished
with parsley.

Spicy Monkfish Brochettes

Culiacin de Rape

2 lb monkfish tail
1 cup water
⅓ cup lime juice

For the sauce
4 red chiles, seeded and
chopped
Olive oil
2 large tomatoes, peeled
and chopped
1 tsp dried oregano
1 tsp freshly ground
black pepper
1 tsp cumin seed
1 tsp ground ginger
2 tsp garlic
2½ cups fish broth
½ large cucumber
1 medium red onion
Lime wedges, to serve
Tabasco sauce, to taste

preparation

For this recipe, you will need six large skewers.

Skin, bone, and cube the fish. Marinate in the water and lime juice for four hours, or overnight if possible.

Fry the chile in a little olive oil, until dark. Add the chopped tomato, oregano, black pepper, cumin seed, ginger, garlic, and fish broth to the chiles. Bring to a boil and simmer for 10 minutes. Remove from the heat.

Cut the cucumber into ¼-inch rounds. Cut the red onion into eighths, by halving like an orange, then quartering each half.

Make up the skewers, by piercing a piece of onion, a piece of fish, a piece of cucumber, etc., until the skewer is full. Coat liberally with the sauce.

Serve with lime wedges and tabasco sauce.

Crab and Brandy Tartlets

Tartas de Cangrejo al Brandy

½ lb piecrust pastry
(see page 24 and halve
the quantity)
½ stick butter
½ medium onion, chopped
fine (preferably a red
onion, as the flavor is
milder)
1 tsp tomato paste
Pinch of sugar
⅔ cup white wine
1 lb crab meat
Pinch of nutmeg
1 Tbsp parsley, chopped
Salt and freshly ground
black pepper
Juice of 2 oranges
1 shot of brandy (about
2 Tbsp)
4 medium eggs and
1 extra yolk
1¼ cups milk (or, for a
richer flavor, use the
same amount of light
cream)
⅔ cup shredded manchego
cheese

preparation

This recipe makes 6 tartlets or one 8-inch flan ring.

Prepare the pastry, rest it, and line the molds thinly. Bake blind: cover the pastry with aluminum foil, fill the case with dried beans and cook in a hot oven (450°F) for 5 to 8 minutes.

to prepare the filling

In a pan, melt the butter. Add the onion and cover. Cook gently until the onion is soft.

Add the tomato paste, sugar, then white wine. Stir in the crab meat, nutmeg, parsley, salt, and pepper. Add the orange juice and brandy, and simmer gently for 5 minutes. Stir and remove from heat. Allow to cool.

In a large bowl, blend the eggs with the milk or cream, whisking well.

Mix the crab mixture and manchego into the milk mix, check the seasoning, and add some freshly ground black pepper.

Spoon the crab mixture into the pastry molds or flan ring. Bake in a moderate oven until golden-brown and set, approximately 15 to 20 minutes.

Note: Manchego cheese is named for the Manchego sheep that grazed the plains of La Mancha, from whose milk it was originally made. It is Spain's most famous cheese. It is semifirm, golden in color, mellow-flavored, and melts beautifully when cooked. It is available in some supermarkets and most specialty cheese stores.

Lobster and Chicken Brochettes

Brochetas de Langosta y Pollo

2 fresh lobsters, each 1½ lb
2 chicken breasts, each 8 oz,
cubed into bite-size
pieces
½ cup dry white wine
½ cup garlic and tomato
mayonnaise

**Garlic and tomato
mayonnaise**
To 1¼ cups mayonnaise add
half its volume plum
tomatoes, canned, and
mix in a food processor,
adding salt, pepper, and
plenty of garlic – 2 tsp
for every 1¼ cups
mayonnaise
Lime wedges, to serve

preparation

You will need 6 skewers for this recipe.

Place the lobsters in a pot of boiling salted water. Lower heat and simmer for 5 minutes, or until they go pink. Remove from pot and allow to cool before handling.

Pull the tail section away from the head with a little twist. Remove the shells and cut the flesh into bite-size chunks.

Poach the chicken pieces in the white wine for 6 to 8 minutes. Cool.

Arrange the lobster and chicken alternately on the skewers.

Serve with the garlic and tomato mayonnaise and lime wedges.

Monkfish and Bacon Brochettes

Brochetas de Rape con Bacon

24 small button mushrooms
9 slices good bacon, sliced in
3-in lengths
1 lb monkfish tail, boned,
skinned, and cubed into
small chunks
Olive oil
Salt and freshly ground
black pepper
½ cup garlic and tomato
mayonnaise (see Lobster
and Chicken Brochettes,
page 19)

preparation

You will need 6 long skewers or 12 smaller sticks for this recipe.

Start by piercing a mushroom on the skewer, then add a piece of folded bacon, then a piece of fish. Repeat until the stick is full and all the ingredients (or sticks) are used up.

Brush with olive oil and season. At this stage you may keep in the refrigerator until needed.

Cook by placing on an oiled cake sheet in a hot oven (425°F) for approximately 7 to 8 minutes, until cooked through.

Dredge with garlic and tomato mayonnaise, and serve.

Smoked Fish Mayonnaise and Garlic Toast

Tostadas con Ajo Cubiertas de Pescado Ahumado

2 green bell peppers

4 Tbsp olive oil

Freshly ground black pepper

1 tomato, peeled and chopped

½ lb smoked mackerel

½ lb smoked cod (you could use cooked salt cod, but if you do, eliminate salt from the seasoning)

½ cup garlic mayonnaise

6 slices of bread or 1 French baguette

1 tsp garlic, crushed

2 Tbsp olive oil

Garlic mayonnaise

Add 2 tsp crushed garlic to 1½ cups mayonnaise and mix in food processor

preparation

Seed the peppers and cut into thin strips. Heat the oil in a pan and stew the peppers over a low heat. Add black pepper and the tomato. Cover and stew for 20 minutes, or until soft. Allow to cool.

Skin and bone the fish, mix the garlic mayonnaise into it, and blend in a food processor with black pepper. It should reach heavy cream consistency; add more garlic mayonnaise if necessary.

Cut the bread into triangles or rounds and toast lightly. Brush on both sides with the garlic and 2 tablespoons olive oil. Bake in a hot oven (425°F), until golden, approximately 3 to 5 minutes.

Spoon a little of the pepper mixture over each of the bread toasties.

Spoon some smoked fish mix onto the pepper and serve—Spanish club sandwich style!

Fish Croquettes

Croquetas de Pescado

12 oz white fish
Enough milk to half-cover the fish (approximately 1 cup)
1½ cups mashed potatoes
¼ cup onion, chopped
Butter, to fry
½ tsp garlic, crushed
½ tsp paprika
1 Tbsp parsley, chopped
1 egg
¼ cup flour
Egg wash (2 eggs beaten with a little milk)
White bread crumbs
Oil or butter, to fry
Lemon wedges and garlic and tomato mayonnaise (see Lobster and Chicken Brochettes, page 19), to serve

preparation

Wash the fish, half-cover with milk and poach in the oven for 15 minutes. Remove all skin, bone, and flake the fish. Set aside.

Prepare the mashed potatoes (both the fish and the potatoes can be prepared in advance).

Soften the onion in a little butter, add the garlic, paprika, and parsley. Stir, and remove from the heat.

Mix the fish, potatoes, and onion together, blending well, and season. Beat in the egg. The resulting mixture should be firm and pliable. Form the mix into little balls. Cover with flour, shake off any excess, and pass through the egg wash to cover completely. Pass through the bread crumbs, reshaping if necessary.

These may be deep-fried in hot oil (365°F) for 3 to 5 minutes until golden, or shallow-fried in melted butter, shaking the pan to brown evenly.

Serve with tomato and garlic mayonnaise and plenty of lemon wedges.

Spinach and Mussel Pot

Mejillones con Espinacas

1 lb spinach
1 medium onion, chopped
½ stick butter
1 tsp garlic, crushed
Pinch of nutmeg
Salt and freshly ground black pepper
⅔ cup dry white wine
3¼ cups chicken broth
2 lb mussels, cleaned (see tip below)
2 Tbsp light cream

preparation

Discard any stalks and large veins if using fresh spinach, and wash thoroughly. Note: it is only necessary to cook fresh spinach. Place in boiling salted water for 2 minutes. Remove and cool under cold water. Squeeze to remove moisture. Chop finely.

Fry the onion in the butter. Add the spinach, garlic, nutmeg, salt, and black pepper. Stir. Add the white wine and turn up the heat. Cook for 5 minutes, until the wine is almost dry. Add the broth and bring to a boil. Stir and cook for 5 minutes. The consistency should be that of heavy cream; if it's too thin, continue cooking over heat, stirring until it thickens.

Add the mussels and cover the pot. Cook until the mussels have opened, continuously shaking the pot. Remove from the heat and season to taste. Pour into bowls, evenly distributing the mussels. Swirl a little cream over each, and serve.

tip

To clean fresh mussels, scrub clean under cold running water, and cut or pull off the long beard. Place in a bowl of cold water and leave to stand for 2 to 3 hours. This will allow the mussels to purge themselves of sand. Discard any that float or are open.

23

Spanish Squid Pie

Empanada de Calamar

For the filling

4 Tbsp olive oil

1 medium onion, chopped

1 tsp garlic, crushed

2 green bell peppers, seeded and cut into fine strips

3 tomatoes, peeled and halved

2 red chiles, seeded and chopped

1 lb squid, cleaned as in recipe for Fried Squid (see page 13)

1 cup fish broth

1 cup red Rioja wine

1 to 2 tsp salt

2 tsp paprika

Sprig of fresh thyme

1 lb mussels, cleaned (see tip, page 23) and simmered in a little boiling salted water for 5 minutes

1 cup shelled shrimp

Salt and freshly ground black pepper

For the pastry

(makes approximately 1 lb pastry)

2 ¼ cups all-purpose flour

Generous ⅛ cup fresh yeast (or ½ oz dried yeast)

1 cup milk, lukewarm

½ stick butter

2 eggs

2 tomatoes, sliced and peeled

1 tsp salt

1 egg yolk mixed with a little milk, to glaze the pie

to prepare the filling

Heat the oil in a large skillet and gently cook the onion and garlic. Add the peppers, tomatoes, and chiles, stir, and cook for 10 minutes.

Add the rings of squid, with the chopped legs. Pour in the broth and red wine, cover, and cook for 20 minutes over a moderate heat. Add the salt, paprika, and thyme; stir. If the mixture looks a little dry, add some water. Remove mussels from the shells and add to the mixture along with shrimp. Remove from heat. Season.

to prepare the pastry

Sift the flour into a bowl and make a well in the center. Crumble or sprinkle the yeast into the well. Pour in the lukewarm milk and stir to dissolve the yeast. Cover with a fine layer of flour. Do not blend this in. Cover the bowl with a cloth and leave the mixture in a warm place to rise until cracks in the covering layer of flour appear, approximately 15 minutes.

While mixture is rising, melt butter in a pan, and beat in eggs. Stir in the salt and cool slightly.

Pour this egg and butter mixture over the floured yeast in the bowl. Stir with a wooden spoon and beat until the dough is thoroughly mixed.

Knead the dough, stretching and pulling with your hands until it is dry and smooth. If it is too soft, add a little more flour. Shape into a ball, place in the bowl, and dust lightly with flour. Cover with a dish cloth. Leave to rise in a warm place for 20 minutes. Knead through again and leave to rise for a further 20 minutes, covered. It is now ready for use.

Grease and line a paella pan (dish for 2) with half the dough. Add the filling; the pie will rise to fill pan. Cover with slices of tomato and a little salt.

Roll out the remaining dough, sealing the edges well. Glaze with the egg yolk and decorate as desired. Leave to stand for 10 minutes before baking.

Bake in the oven at 400°F for 30 minutes. Leave to cool, and slice to serve.

Russian Salad

Ensaladilla Rusa

8 medium potatoes
1 medium carrot, cut into cubes
1 cup fresh peas
2 hard-cooked eggs, cooled, peeled, and cut into cubes
One 7 oz can water-packed tuna, drained, and flaked
1 red bell pepper, cut into cubes
½ cup corn
½ cup black olives
1½ cups mayonnaise

preparation

Put the potatoes in a large saucepan of water and bring to a boil. Cover, lower the heat, and simmer for about 20 to 25 minutes, or until the potatoes are done. Drain, and when cool, cut into ¼-inch cubes.

Boil the carrot and peas for 3 to 5 minutes, until lightly cooked. Drain.

Mix the potato with the egg, tuna, carrot, peas, pepper, corn, and olives in a large salad bowl.

Just before serving, add the mayonnaise to the salad, and toss to coat.

Mussels and Beans with Tomato

Mejillones con Judías en Salsa de Tomate

2 lb white navy beans
2 Tbsp olive oil
1 medium onion, chopped
2 slices good bacon, chopped
2 tsp garlic, crushed
5 cups chicken broth
2 lb mussels, cleaned (see tip, page 23)
1 large tomato, peeled and chopped
1 Tbsp parsley, chopped
Juice of 1 lemon
Salt and freshly ground black pepper

preparation

Soak the beans overnight in cold water, or buy ready-to-cook beans.

Heat the oil and fry the onion in it until soft. Add the bacon and stir. Add the beans and garlic, cover with the chicken broth, and cook (20 minutes for canned beans, 2 hours for dried, soaked beans).

Add the mussels, shake, cover, and cook until the mussels open. Stir in the tomato, parsley, and lemon juice. Season and serve in small bowls.

Anchovy and Mussels in White Wine Sauce

Mejillones con Anchoas San Sebastián

2 medium onions, chopped
2 green bell peppers, seeded
and chopped fine
½ cup olive oil
1 tsp garlic, crushed
1 Tbsp paprika
1 lb fresh anchovies, or
1 lb frozen smelt,
defrosted
1 cup dry white wine
1 cup white wine vinegar
1¼ cups fish broth
2 lb mussels, cleaned
(see tip, page 23)

preparation

Fry the onions and peppers in the olive oil. Add the garlic and paprika, stir, and add the fish. Simmer for approximately 5 minutes.

Pour on the wine, vinegar, and broth, and bring to a boil. Add the mussels. Cover and cook, until the mussels open.

Season and serve in shallow dishes.

Fried Stuffed Mussels

Mejillones Fritos

1 medium onion, chopped
½ stick butter
1¼ cups dry white wine
2 parsley sprigs
Zest of 1 lemon
36 mussels (about 2 lb),
cleaned (see tip,
page 23)
5 oz cured ham (Spanish
jamón serrano or
Italian prosciutto)
1 cup soft white bread
crumbs
⅔ cup grated Parmesan
cheese
Salt and freshly ground
black pepper
2 Tbsp parsley, chopped

For the béchamel sauce
¾ stick butter
⅔ cup flour
1¼ cups milk
Salt and freshly ground
black pepper

preparation

Fry the onion in the butter in a pot. Add the wine, parsley stalks, and lemon zest, and bring to a boil. Add the mussels, cover, and shake pot over high heat until the shells open. Remove the mussels with a slotted spoon and place in a bowl to cool. Strain the cooking liquid and keep it to add to the béchamel.

Remove the mussels from the shells (keeping the shells to one side). Grind the mussels with the ham or, if you prefer, wrap the mussels in small squares of ham. With a teaspoon put back into the shells, leaving space for the sauce.

to prepare the béchamel sauce

Melt the butter; stir in the flour. Warm 1¼ cups milk and add gradually, beating with a wooden spoon. Add the mussel liquid and simmer for 20 minutes. Season. The sauce should be quite thick. Spread the béchamel over the mussels and ham in the shells with a spoon or small palette knife. It will seal the mixture.

Mix the bread crumbs with the cheese, and season. Sprinkle over the shells, place under a hot broiler, and broil until the cheese melts. Serve immediately, garnished with parsley.

Mussel, Shrimp, and Squid Tapa

Ensalada de Marisco

3 cups fish broth

2 cups white wine

1 lb fresh shrimp in shell

2 lb mussels, cleaned (see tip, page 23)

2 Tbsp olive oil

3 tsp garlic, crushed

3 tsp paprika

1 lb squid, cleaned and blanched (as in recipe for Fried Squid, page 13)

½ cup lemon juice

Salt and freshly ground black pepper

Parsley, to garnish

preparation

In a saucepan, bring the broth and wine to a boil. Add the shrimp and cook for 2 minutes. Remove from the pan with a slotted spoon, and drain.

Add the mussels to the broth, cover, and cook until the shells open. Remove from the pan with a slotted spoon, and drain.

Heat the oil in another pan and add the garlic and paprika. Cook for 2 minutes, stirring continuously. Add the shrimp, mussels, squid, and lemon juice to the pan, season well, and stir to mix all the ingredients. Heat through for 2 minutes and serve immediately, garnished with parsley.

Giant Shrimp in Garlic

Langostinos al Ajillo

3 Tbsp olive oil
12 giant shrimp, fresh if
available; if not, cook
from frozen
2 tsp garlic, crushed
2 tsp paprika
2 Tbsp medium sherry
Lemon wedges, to serve

preparation

Heat the oil in a pot. For frozen shrimp, lower heat, add the shrimp to the oil, cover and cook for 6 minutes, until soft and heated through. For fresh shrimp, add to the oil and cook until sizzling.

Add the rest of the ingredients and bring to a boil. Taste for seasoning and serve with lemon wedges.

Shrimp Salad

Ceviche de Gambas

2 lb shrimp or 1 lb shrimp
and 1 lb white fish

5 cups water

2½ cups lime juice

2 medium red onions,
chopped fine

2 Tbsp soy sauce

Salt and freshly ground
black pepper

2 cucumbers, seeded and cut
into cubes

1 red bell pepper, seeded and
cut into cubes

1 bunch of dill, chopped

Tabasco sauce, to taste

Lime wedges, to serve

preparation

Shell and devein shrimp, and skin and clean fish (if using). Place in a large bowl.

Mix the ingredients for the marinade together (water, lime juice, red onions, soy sauce, salt, and pepper) and pour over the shrimp. Marinate for 20 minutes.

Add the cucumber, pepper slices, and dill. Toss together in the bowl.

Spoon onto plates or into small bowls. Sprinkle with pepper and tabasco sauce. Serve with lime wedges.

Glazed Giant Shrimp

Langostinos Glaseados

12 giant shrimp; if frozen, defrost
2 egg yolks
1¼ cups mayonnaise
1 Tbsp heavy cream
Freshly ground black pepper
½ tsp paprika
1 tomato, skinned and chopped into small squares
3 tsp garlic, crushed
Oil, to brush cookie sheet
1 Tbsp parsley, chopped
Lemon or lime wedges and garlic bread (see Garlic Bread, page 40), to serve

preparation

Carefully remove the shell from the tails of the shrimp, keeping the heads intact.

Whisk the yolks into the mayonnaise with the heavy cream, black pepper, paprika, tomato, and garlic.

Heat the broiler and brush a cookie sheet with oil.

Place the shrimp on the cookie sheet and spoon the mayonnaise mixture over the tails.

Heat under the broiler until brown spots appear.

Sprinkle the shrimp with the chopped parsley and serve immediately with lemon or lime wedges and garlic bread.

Giant Shrimp with Egg and Anchovy

Langostinos con Huevo y Anchoas

6 cooked giant shrimp, peeled (it is optional to remove the heads)
3 hard-cooked eggs, shelled and halved
6 anchovy fillets
6 black olives
¾ cup mayonnaise

preparation

You will need 6 cocktail sticks for this recipe.

On each stick, spear 1 shrimp tail, half a cooked egg, a rolled anchovy filet, and a black olive. Either cover in mayonnaise, or serve as a dip.

Bacon-wrapped Shrimp with Sour Cream

Langostinos Envueltos en Tocineta

12 giant shrimp, shelled,
leaving on the head and
tail tip (defrost overnight
if using frozen)
½ cup shredded fresh
mozzarella cheese
1 tsp freshly ground black
pepper
12 slices good bacon,
trimmed of the rind
and excess fat
A little olive oil

For the sauce/dip
1 cup sour cream
½ tsp each salt and freshly
ground black pepper
Juice of ½ lemon

preparation

Make a slit lengthwise along the back of the shrimp, but do not cut through. Fill the slit with the cheese, mixed with the black pepper.

Wrap each shrimp in one strip of bacon; start at the head, which should peep out, and slightly spiral the bacon to the tail. Secure with small skewers if necessary. Paint with olive oil, and either broil or bake in a hot oven (450°F) for 7 to 10 minutes. Meanwhile, prepare the dip.

to prepare the sauce/dip

Mix all the ingredients together for the sauce, and serve with the hot shrimp.

Oysters with Lime and Tabasco

Ostras Picantes con Lima

12 large fresh oysters
Tabasco sauce
Juice of 4 limes
Freshly ground black pepper
Lime wedges, to serve

preparation

Ask your fishmonger to shuck (open) your oysters for you. If this is not possible, follow the preparation instructions below.

Brush oysters under cold running water to clean. Place each oyster on a heavy chopping board, with the flat side up, and hit gently with a hammer to break off the thin edge of the shell.

Slide an oyster knife into the back of the shell and sever the hinge close to the flat upper shell. Remove upper shell and discard.

Cut the oyster from the lower shell and pick out any pieces of shell or grit. Place cleaned oyster in deep lower shell. Add 2 drops of tabasco sauce to each one. Sprinkle with lime juice and black pepper to serve.

Oysters Bloody Mary

Ostras Bloody Mary

1½ cups tomato juice
3 Tbsp vodka
5 drops Tabasco sauce
1 tsp Worcestershire sauce
1 Tbsp lemon juice
Salt and freshly ground
black pepper
12 oysters
Cucumber, cut into cubes
Celery stalks (small, young
ones), cut into cubes
Lemon wedges, to serve

preparation

Mix a Bloody Mary using the tomato juice, vodka,
Tabasco sauce, Worcestershire sauce, lemon juice, salt,
and pepper; mix in a blender with some ice cubes so it
is well chilled.

Open the oysters carefully (see page 34), and fill the
shells with the Bloody Mary mix.

Sprinkle the cubed cucumber and celery over the
shells, and serve with lemon wedges.

Vegetable Tapas

Asparagus and Lettuce Tarts

Tartas de Esparragos con Lechuga

1 lb asparagus, fresh, or
1 lb can of asparagus
spears
Juice of 1 lemon
1 medium onion, chopped
fine
½ stick butter
½ medium lettuce
1 clove garlic, crushed
Salt and freshly ground
black pepper
2 Tbsp dry white wine
½ lb piecrust pastry
(see page 24 and halve
the quantity)
1¼ cups light cream
4 eggs and 1 extra egg yolk
½ cup cheese, preferably
manchego (see note
page 18), shredded

One 8-in flan ring or
tart-pan, or 10 tartlet
molds

preparation

If using fresh asparagus, discard the stringy white root part and chop the rest into ½-inch pieces. Keep the tips separate.

Place the chopped asparagus in a pot of boiling salted water with the lemon juice added; keep back the tips. Simmer 8 to 10 minutes until just soft, adding the tips after 5 minutes. Remove from the heat, place a strainer over the pot, and run cold water through it over the sink. The strainer will save the asparagus tips from breaking up into small pieces.

If using canned asparagus, drain well, and check that it is evenly chopped.

Gently cook the onion in the butter, covered, until soft. Add the finely chopped lettuce to the onion and stir. Add the garlic and seasoning. Pour in the white wine, stir, and cook until the lettuce softens. If you need more liquid, add a little water. Cover and simmer for 5 minutes. Remove from the heat and allow to cool before mixing the asparagus with the onion and lettuce.

Grease and flour 10 tartlet molds, or one 8-inch flan ring, and position the pastry. Bake blind: cover the pastry with aluminum foil, fill the case with baking beans or rice, and cook in a hot oven (450°F) for 5 to 8 minutes. Remove the foil and beans.

Mix the cream with the eggs, and some salt and black pepper. Whisk well to break the egg white. Whisk in the shredded cheese. Stir the lettuce and asparagus mix into the cream and egg mix, thoroughly blending the two so that the mix coats the vegetables. Spoon into the pastry molds, placing the tips on top.

Cook in a moderate oven (350°F) for 10 minutes for tartlets or 15 minutes for flan-size.

The filling should be just firm to the touch and golden-brown when ready.

Eggplant with Cheese and Shrimp

Berenjenas Rellenas de Gambas y Queso

1 large eggplant
Salt
½ cup flour
Olive oil
1¼ cups thick cheese sauce
(see below)
Parsley, to garnish

For the cheese sauce
½ stick butter
¼ cup flour
1¼ cups milk, warmed
½ small onion, chopped
1 bay leaf
Pinch of nutmeg
⅔ cup shredded manchego
or Parmesan cheese
1 Tbsp light cream
1 egg yolk
1 cup shelled shrimp
Salt and freshly ground
black pepper

preparation

Slice the eggplant into thin rounds, spread the slices in a large tray, and sprinkle with salt. Leave for 20 minutes to remove excess moisture. Pat dry with a paper towel and pass through the flour, shaking off any excess.

Pour enough olive oil in a large skillet to cover the base, and heat. Place the floured eggplant rounds into the oil and fry on each side until golden. Remove and drain on paper towels or waxed paper. Arrange carefully and keep to one side.

to prepare the cheese sauce

Melt the butter in a pan. Stir in the flour and cook gently to a paste. Add the warmed milk gradually, stirring all the time until smooth. Add the onion, bay leaf, and nutmeg, and heat gently for 20 minutes to cook the flour. Pass through a strainer. Stir in the cheese and the cream. Remove from the heat and beat in the egg yolk. Season. Mix the shrimp into the sauce.

Arrange the eggplant slices on a cookie sheet. Spoon over the cheese and shrimp sauce. Sprinkle with the Parmesan and cook in a hot oven (400°F) until golden-brown. Garnish with parsley and serve.

Cheese and Potato Croquettes

Croquetas de Patata y Queso

2 lb potatoes
2 egg yolks
½ stick butter
Salt and freshly ground black pepper
Pinch of nutmeg
Dash of sherry
½ cup shredded Parmesan cheese
Pinch of dry mustard
2 Tbsp parsley, chopped
Seasoned flour
Egg wash (2 eggs beaten with a little milk)
Bread crumbs
Parsley, to garnish

preparation

Wash and peel the potatoes, and cut to an even size. Cook in salted water until soft; then drain. Put a lid on the pan of the potatoes and place over a low heat to dry out, stirring occasionally to prevent burning.

Place the potatoes in a food processor with the yolks, butter, and seasoning. Mix in the nutmeg, sherry, Parmesan cheese, mustard, and parsley. The potatoes should be like a very firm mash. Overmixing will make them gluey, in which case some flour will have to be worked in by hand.

Check the mix is well seasoned and mold into cylinder shapes, measuring 5 by 2 inches. Roll in seasoned flour, dip in egg wash, and coat with bread crumbs.

Deep-fry in hot fat (365°F). When golden, drain well and serve garnished with parsley.

Note: If you want to keep the croquettes for cooking later, or the next day, place them carefully on a tray, cover with plastic wrap, and refrigerate.

Garlic Bread

Pan de Ajo

3 cloves garlic
2 sticks butter, softened to
room temperature
1 Tbsp parsley, chopped
Salt and freshly ground
black pepper
1 large crusty loaf, or
6 small pita breads

preparation

Peel the garlic by placing on a cake sheet in a hot oven (450°F) for 10 minutes (the garlic will pop out of its skin). Crush the peeled garlic cloves in a crusher, food processor, or by the old-fashioned method of crushing under the blade of a large knife, with salt. Blend the crushed garlic into the butter. Add the chopped parsley and seasoning.

Place the bread in a hot oven (450°F) for 15 minutes. If using pita breads, sprinkle with a little water before placing in the oven to give a softer bread. Slice the loaf, smother with the butter, and serve.

There are several savory alternatives to this recipe:

Add 2 teaspoons of tomato paste to the butter, smother bread with the pink butter, and toast.

Use 1 1/2 sticks butter and 1/2 cup shredded cheese, in place of the 2 sticks butter. Mix together with the flavorings. Heat the bread, slice, smother with the butter-cheese mix, and place back in the oven to melt the cheese. Season and serve.

Garlic Mushrooms

Champiñones al Ajillo

3/4 stick butter
1 1/2 lb mushrooms, button
or cap
A few drops of lemon juice
Salt and freshly ground
black pepper
3 tsp garlic, crushed
1 Tbsp cilantro or parsley,
chopped

preparation

Heat the butter in a large pan. Add the mushrooms and cook gently, covered, for 5 minutes, shaking occasionally.

Add the lemon juice, salt, and pepper, and increase the heat, tossing the mushrooms well. Add the garlic, toss, and cook for 2 minutes.

Add the cilantro or parsley and cook for 1 minute. Remove from the heat and serve.

Stewed Giant Olives

Aceitunas Gigantes

1 jar large olives, cut around
the pit without cutting
through
1 medium onion, chopped
1 clove garlic, peeled and
part crushed
1 bay leaf
2 Tbsp olive oil
2 Tbsp red wine vinegar

preparation

This recipe makes 5 cups of olives.

Put the ingredients in a pan. Cover with water, adding enough olive oil to put a slick on the top. Bring to a boil and simmer, covered, until soft, for 4 to 6 hours.

These will keep well in the refrigerator for 2 weeks.

Three Peppers in Tomato and Garlic

Pimientos en Tomate y Ajo

2 yellow bell peppers
2 red bell peppers
2 green bell peppers
¾ cup olive oil
1 Tbsp parsley, chopped
2 tsp garlic, crushed
8 oz of fresh tomatoes, preferably small, or 8 oz canned tomatoes
Salt and freshly ground black pepper

preparation

Seed the bell peppers and cut into thin strips. Heat the oil in a large skillet and cook the peppers gently for 2 to 3 minutes, stirring frequently. Add the parsley and garlic and cook for another couple of minutes.

Add the chopped tomatoes and their juice to the pan. Stir and season. Cover the pan and simmer gently for about 20 minutes, until the peppers are tender.

The sauce should be quite thick—if necessary, remove the peppers and boil rapidly to reduce the liquid. Check the seasoning.

This is a summer *tapa*, and may be eaten hot or cold; its flavor improves after one day.

Note: If you like spicy food, substitute chili oil for the olive oil.

Cold Soup

G a z p a c h o

¾ cup white bread crumbs
¼ cup olive oil
1 cucumber, peeled and chopped
1 green bell pepper, seeded
8 oz of fresh tomatoes, skinned and chopped
1 medium onion
1 tsp garlic, crushed
1 Tbsp lemon juice
Salt and freshly ground black pepper

preparation

Using a fork, mix the bread crumbs and olive oil in a bowl to form a smooth paste.

Blend the remaining ingredients in a food processor, stir in the bread paste, season well, and chill.

If you prefer a more liquid soup, add tomato juice and stir well.

Stuffed Bell Peppers with Ground Chili Beef

P i m i e n t a s   V e r d e s   c o n   P i c a n t e

1 lb ground beef or pork
¼ cup oil (or ½ stick butter)
1 onion, chopped fine
2 tsp garlic, crushed
6 red chiles, chopped fine
½ tsp dried oregano
1 bay leaf
2½ cups water
Salt and freshly ground black pepper
2 tsp tomato paste
1 tsp basil, chopped
8 oz can kidney beans
2 large tomatoes, peeled and chopped
3 large or 6 small green bell peppers
½ cup shredded manchego cheese (see note, page 18)

to prepare the filling

Gently cook the meat in the oil or butter. Add the onion, garlic, chiles, oregano, bay leaf, water, salt, pepper, tomato paste, and basil, and cook, stirring, until it comes to a boil. Lower heat and simmer for 45 minutes, stirring occasionally. Add the beans and tomato, season to taste, and bring to a boil. Remove from heat.

to prepare the peppers

Remove the stalks. Plunge into boiling salted water and simmer for 5 minutes. Immediately cool in cold water and drain.

For large peppers, cut in half lengthwise, and seed. Fill with meat mixture, sprinkle with cheese, and bake at 400°F until the cheese melts. For small peppers, cut off the tops, and place aside. Carefully seed, core, and trim the bases without making holes in them, so the peppers sit squarely. Fill with meat and cheese. Place on a cookie sheet with the top next to it and bake at 400°F until the cheese melts. Replace tops and serve.

43

Stuffed Tomatoes

Tomates Rellenos

8 small tomatoes, or 3 large
tomatoes
4 hard-cooked eggs, cooled
and peeled
6 Tbsp garlic mayonnaise
(see Smoked Fish
Mayonnaise and Garlic
Toast, page 21)
Salt and freshly ground
black pepper
1 Tbsp parsley, chopped
1 Tbsp white bread crumbs,
if using large tomatoes

preparation

Skin the tomatoes, first by cutting out the core with a
sharp knife and making a '+' incision on the other end
of the tomato. Then place in a pan of boiling water
for 10 seconds, remove and plunge into a bowl of iced
or very cold water (this latter step is to stop the
tomatoes from cooking and going mushy).

Slice the tops off the tomatoes, and just enough of
their bases to remove the rounded ends so that they
will sit squarely on the plate. Keep the tops if using
small tomatoes, but discard those of large tomatoes.
Remove the seeds and insides, either with a teaspoon
or small, sharp knife.

Mash the eggs with the mayonnaise, salt, pepper, and
parsley. Stuff the tomatoes, firmly pressing the filling
down. With small tomatoes, replace the lids at a
jaunty angle. If keeping to serve later, brush them
with olive oil and black pepper to prevent them from
drying out. Cover with plastic wrap and keep.

For large tomatoes, the filling must be firm enough to
be sliced. If you make your own mayonnaise, thicken
it by using more egg yolks. If you use store-bought
mayonnaise, add white bread crumbs until the
mixture reaches the consistency of mashed potatoes.
Season. Fill the tomatoes, pressing down firmly until
level. Refrigerate for 1 hour, then slice with a sharp
carving knife into rings. Sprinkle with chopped parsley.

Tomato Salad with Olives

Ensalada de Tomate con Aceitunas

3 large tomatoes
½ medium red onion, sliced fine
A few black olives
Chives, to garnish

preparation

Slice the tomatoes horizontally. Arrange either in a large bowl with onion in between layers, or spread out on a large plate. Sprinkle with black olives.

For the vinaigrette
½ cup olive oil
3 Tbsp red wine vinegar
½ tsp garlic, chopped fine
½ Tbsp sugar
Salt and freshly ground black pepper

to prepare the vinaigrette

Combine the olive oil, red wine vinegar, garlic, and sugar in a bottle with a screw top. Shake hard until the dressing is emulsified. Add salt and pepper to taste, and shake again. Dredge the tomatoes with the dressing and serve garnished with chopped chives.

If keeping to serve later, add the vinaigrette 20 minutes before required. The vinaigrette will keep in the refrigerator for up to two weeks.

Artichoke Hearts with Tomato and Lemon

Alcachofas con Tomate
y Limón

6 artichokes
Juice of 1 lemon
1 tsp flour
2½ cups cold water
Salt

preparation

Cut off the artichoke stalks and pull out the underneath leaves. With a large knife, cut through the artichoke, leaving only about 1 inch at the bottom of the vegetable.

For the sauce
¾ stick butter
1 small onion, chopped fine
1 tsp garlic, crushed
4 slices good bacon or smoked ham, chopped
8 oz can plum tomatoes or 2 large tomatoes, skinned, seeded, and chopped
2 Tbsp parsley, chopped
Salt and freshly ground pepper
Juice of 2 lemons
The 6 cooked artichoke bottoms

While holding the artichoke upside down, peel carefully with a small paring knife, removing all the leaf and any green part, and keeping the bottom as smooth as possible. If necessary, smooth with a peeler. Immediately rub with lemon and keep in lemon water.

Use a teaspoon or your thumb to remove the furry choke in the center. It should come out easily. If you have problems, don't worry: it will come out easily after cooking, though it will be a little messy. Discard.

Mix the flour and water together, then add the salt and lemon juice. Pass through a strainer into a pan and bring to a boil, stirring constantly. Add the artichokes. Simmer gently until just tender, for about 20 minutes. Drain.

to prepare the sauce

Take the artichoke bottoms and cut into 5 or 6 triangles, by cutting each one in half, then each half into 2 or 3.

Melt the butter in a pan. Add the onion, garlic, and bacon, and cook gently for 5 minutes.

Add the tomato and parsley. Season and bring to a boil. Pour in the lemon juice. Add the artichoke bottom pieces. Heat gently, stirring. If the mix is too tart, add a pinch of sugar.

Serve with crusty bread and a tomato salad.

Pickled Cucumber with Chiles

Conserva de Pepinillos con Picante

2 cucumbers
Salt
2 red chiles, or 1 Tbsp chili oil
1 tsp garlic, crushed
Freshly ground black pepper
White wine vinegar
Sugar

preparation

Peel the cucumbers and slice finely. Spread on a tray and sprinkle with salt to remove the excess moisture. Leave for 2 hours.

Wash the salt off the cucumbers, and drain.

Chop the chiles, discarding the seeds. Mix the chiles with the cucumber and garlic, seasoning with freshly ground black pepper.

Place in a jar, preferably one with a screw-top. Cover with white wine vinegar and enough sugar to remove the acidity. Stir well and cover.

This may be eaten the next day—or even a year hence.

Mint and Chile Cucumber

Pepinillos con Picante y Menta

1 cucumber
1 large tomato
½ tsp garlic, chopped
Bunch of mint, chopped
Small container of plain yogurt
Small container of sour cream
1 tsp ground cumin
2 red chiles, seeded and chopped
Salt and freshly ground black pepper

preparation

Shred the cucumber, sprinkle with salt, and put aside in a strainer while you prepare the other ingredients.

Peel the tomato by placing in boiling water for 10 seconds and then plunging into iced or very cold water to loosen the skin. Chop into little squares and discard the seeds.

Wash the excess moisture off the cucumber and drain well, squeezing out any moisture.

Mix all the ingredients together in a bowl, season well, and chill before serving.

Green Beans Tapa

Tapa de Judías Verdes

1 lb green beans, tops
removed
½ stick butter
¼ cup olive oil
½ medium onion, chopped
fine
Salt and freshly ground
black pepper
1¼ cups chicken broth
1 Tbsp garlic, crushed

preparation

Place the beans in a pot of boiling salted water and cook for 6 to 8 minutes, until the beans are no longer raw but remain fairly firm. Drain well.

Melt the butter in a pan, add the olive oil, and heat. Add the onion and cook gently for 3 to 4 minutes. Add the beans, salt, and pepper, and toss together. Add the chicken broth and the garlic. Cover and cook until tender, approximately 10 minutes. Season well and serve.

Stuffed Zucchini

Calabacin Estofado

6 small zucchini
½ medium onion, chopped fine
1 Tbsp olive oil
½ lb lamb, ground
3 slices good bacon, chopped fine
Salt and freshly ground black pepper
1 tsp tomato paste
½ tsp sugar
1 tsp garlic, crushed
1 Tbsp water
1 tomato, peeled and chopped
½ small container plain yogurt
12 mint leaves, chopped
¼ cup shredded Parmesan cheese
Extra chopped mint, to garnish

preparation

Trim off the ends of the zucchini and discard. Place the zucchini in boiling salted water for 5 minutes. Cut in half lengthwise and, with a teaspoon, scoop out the seeds along the center.

Gently cook the onion in the oil until soft. Add the ground lamb, bacon, salt, and pepper. Stir. Add the tomato paste, sugar, garlic, and water. Cook until the meat is cooked through, for about 15 minutes.

Stir in the tomato, yogurt, and mint leaves. Spoon this mix into the hollowed-out zucchini.

Sprinkle with the Parmesan cheese and black pepper. Bake in a hot oven (400°F) until the cheese melts. Sprinkle with the remaining mint leaves and serve.

Zucchini with Dill

Calabacines a las Hierbas

¼ cup olive oil
¼ stick butter
1 onion, chopped
1 tsp garlic, crushed
1 lb zucchini, topped, tailed, and sliced in thick rounds
½ tsp freshly ground black pepper
2 tsp paprika
1 Tbsp dill, chopped (not the stalks)
Salt, to taste

preparation

Heat oil and butter in a large skillet. Gently cook the onion and garlic until soft. Turn up the heat, add the zucchini and black pepper, and toss.

Cook for 5 to 10 minutes, turning the zucchini slices to cook both sides.

When the zucchini slices are browning, add the paprika and dill. Season and serve.

Roast Potatoes in Sweet Hot Sauce

Patatas Bravas

1 onion, chopped
2 Tbsp olive oil
1 bay leaf
2 red chiles
2 tsp garlic
1 Tbsp tomato paste
½ Tbsp sugar (up to 1 Tbsp, if the sauce is too tart for your liking)
1 Tbsp soy sauce
1 lb can plum tomatoes, chopped
⅔ cup white wine
Salt and freshly ground black pepper
8 medium potatoes

to prepare the sauce

Gently cook the onions in the oil with the bay leaf. When soft, add the chiles, garlic, tomato paste, sugar, and soy sauce. Cook for a further 5 minutes on a low heat.

Add the chopped tomatoes and white wine. Stir and bring to a boil. Simmer for 10 minutes. Season to taste. This sauce should be slightly sweet; the flavor of the tomatoes should not dominate it.

to prepare the potatoes

Cut the potatoes like small roast potatoes.

Grease a cake sheet. Season the potatoes well and brush with melted butter. Roast in a hot oven (450°F) until golden.

Pour the tomato sauce over the potatoes and serve.

Garlic Potatoes

Patatas al Alioli

8 medium potatoes
2 egg yolks
1 tsp crushed garlic
2 tsp vinegar
⅛ tsp mustard
Salt and freshly ground black pepper
1½ cups olive oil
Approximately 2 tsp boiling water

preparation

Prepare the potatoes as for Roast Potatoes in Sweet Hot Sauce (see above).

Place yolks, garlic, vinegar, mustard, and seasoning in a bowl or food processor. Gradually pour on the oil, very slowly, whisking, or whizzing continually. Add the boiling water, whisking well. Pour the dressing over the potatoes, stir to mix, and serve.

Refried Kidney Beans

Habitas Refritas

1 lb can kidney beans
1 red chile, seeded and
chopped
1 medium onion, chopped
fine
2 tsp garlic, crushed
1 tsp paprika
Salt and freshly ground
black pepper
5 cups water
6 slices good bacon, without
the rind
½ stick butter
Parsley, to serve

preparation

Place first 7 ingredients in a pan, bring to a boil, and simmer for 40 minutes.

Place one-quarter of the total in a food processor and purée. Remix the puréed beans with the whole beans.

Chop the bacon and place in boiling water for 10 minutes to remove the saltiness. Remove from the water and drain.

Heat the butter in a skillet and fry the bacon. Add the beans, little by little, and mash with the back of a spoon. Season well.

The beans should go into a thick purée. Season, sprinkle with parsley, and serve. The more often you refry the beans, the better they taste.

Stuffed Cabbage Leaves

Repollo Estofado

1 large green cabbage, or
1 lb spinach
1 tsp paprika
Salt and freshly ground
black pepper
½ Tbsp parsley, chopped
1 lb lamb, ground
½ stick butter
1 onion, chopped fine
1 tsp garlic, crushed
1 red chile, seeded
and chopped
1 tsp tomato paste
1 cup tomato juice
1 tsp soy sauce
1¼ cups chicken broth
½ cup mushrooms,
chopped fine
⅜ cup salted peanuts,
crushed

preparation

Remove the dirty outer leaves from the cabbage. Carefully pick off the large whole leaves and cut out the thick part of the stalk. Put the leaves in a pot of boiling salted water to soften. Simmer for 5 minutes.

Remove the leaves and plunge into cold water. When cold, carefully lay out the leaves on a clean dishcloth or paper towel, and pat dry with another dishcloth placed on top. Arrange with the inside of the leaves facing toward you.

to prepare the filling

In a large bowl work the paprika, salt, pepper, and parsley into the ground lamb.

Melt the butter in a pan. Add the onion and cook gently until softened. Add the lamb, garlic, chile, and tomato paste. Pour in the tomato juice, soy sauce, and broth, and stir. Add the mushrooms and peanuts.

Simmer for 30 minutes, stirring occasionally. Remove from the heat and cool. Check the seasoning. If the mixture is still runny, add a small amount of flour.

When cold, spoon small amounts of the mixture into the center of the cabbage leaves, folding the outside edges over and placing the folded side, base down, in an oiled baking pan.

Note: If your leaves are a little ragged or small, use two leaves to wrap around the lamb mixture.

When all the cabbage parcels are in the baking pan, pour in enough chicken broth to half-cover them. Cover the tray with aluminum foil. Pierce with a fork to allow the steam to escape and poach in the oven for 20 minutes, at 400°F.

Remove carefully with a large spoon and moisten with a little of the poaching liquor.

opposite: Stuffed Cabbage Leaves

Corn on the Cob with Garlic Butter

Mazorca con Mantequilla de Ajo

4 fresh corn on the cob
Garlic butter (see recipe for
Garlic Bread, page 40)
Salt and freshly ground
black pepper

preparation

Shuck the fresh corn. Place in boiling salted water with a drop of olive oil. Simmer for 20 minutes, or until the corn is cooked and tender.

Remove from the heat and drain. Smother liberally with garlic butter, season well, and serve.

Egg & Cheese

Huevos y Quesos

Goat Cheese with Tarragon and Garlic Marinade

Queso de Cabra con Ajo y Estragón

Goat cheese

For the marinade
4½ cups olive oil
1 Tbsp white wine vinegar
1 bunch of tarragon, with crushed stalks
1 bulb of garlic
Black peppercorns

preparation

Try to get genuine manchego cheese (see note, page 18) for this recipe. If this is not possible, use a mild, milky flavored goat cheese.

Leaving the rind on the cheese, chop it into even bite-size chunks.

Mix together the ingredients for the marinade. Cover and refrigerate the cheese, and leave for at least 4 days in a jar or porcelain pot before eating.

Chile with Manchego Cheese

Quejo Manchego con Salsa Picante

6 red chiles, seeded and chopped
1 cup olive oil
Salt and freshly ground black pepper
2 cups manchego cheese (see note, page 18)
Lime wedges, to serve

preparation

Blend the chiles with the olive oil, adding a good pinch each of salt and pepper.

Cut the cheese into small cubes.

Pour the oil over the cheese and marinate for at least 2 hours. Serve with lime wedges and toothpicks.

Spanish Omelet

Tortilla Española

Basic recipe for 1 omelet
*3 potatoes (or an equal
amount of potato to
onion)*
3 Tbsp olive oil
*1 onion, chopped fine or
sliced*
*Salt and freshly ground
black pepper*
3 eggs
Chives, to garnish

preparation

Note: When frying, if the mixture becomes a little too dry, add more oil.

Wash the potatoes. (It is optional to peel them— Spaniards will never put unpeeled potato in an omelet, but other people like to.) Slice very finely and place in a pot of cold salted water. Bring to a boil and cook for 5 minutes (parboil). If preferred, the potatoes for this dish can be sautéed.

Place a skillet on the heat and heat the oil. Add the onion carefully, as the oil might spit. Stir while cooking. Add the potato slices. Shake the pan, and stir to prevent any sticking to the bottom. Season lightly with salt and pepper.

In a bowl, beat the eggs, and season well.

Lower the heat slightly under the potatoes and onion and cook, tossing until golden-brown. Add the potato and onion to the egg mix, and stir well. Replace the pan on the heat and when hot pour the mixture into it. It will seal immediately. Cook for 2 minutes, then turn the omelet by one of 2 methods: either slip the omelet into another hot pan brushed with oil by placing pan no. 2 over pan no. 1 and flip it; or place a large plate over the omelet, flip the omelet onto the plate, and slide it back into the pan so the uncooked side is now over the heat. Cook for 1 minute.

Leave to cool, garnish with chives, and slice to serve. The omelet should be thick, firm, and cake-like, quite unlike the French omelet.

Note: Many ingredients and flavorings may be used (or used up!) in omelets, for instance, green bell peppers (sliced and added to the onions), mushrooms, cooked ham, cheese, and so on.

opposite: Spanish Omelet

Egg and Garlic Fried Bread

Pan Frito con Ajo y Huevo

3 eggs
A few drops of warm water
2 tsp garlic, crushed
Salt and freshly ground
black pepper
3 Tbsp olive oil
6 slices of bread

preparation

Beat the eggs in a bowl with a few drops of warm water. Add the crushed garlic and seasoning to the egg and mix well.

Heat the oil in a skillet. Dip the bread in the egg so that both sides are covered, and place in the skillet. Fry until each side is golden brown.

Note: The oil must be hot for this recipe to seal the egg immediately (watch for a wavy look on the pan bottom). Also, the bread must be turned quickly to prevent the garlic from burning.

Paella Croquettes

Croquetas de Paella

2 cups short-grain rice
1 medium onion, chopped rough
1 bay leaf
1 tsp garlic, crushed
1 chicken broth cube
1 Tbsp olive oil
2 tsp turmeric
2 times the quantity of water to rice (ideally, use good chicken broth)
10 oz chorizo sausage and smoked ham, mixed, preferably in equal quantities (any spiced salamis or cooked meats may be used for this recipe)
Seasoned flour
Egg wash (2 eggs, beaten with a little milk)
Bread crumbs
Oil, to fry
Parsley, to serve

preparation

Put the rice in a pot, and add the onion, bay leaf, garlic, stock, olive oil, and turmeric. Pour the hot water over the mix.

Put on the heat and bring the mix to a boil. Turn down the heat and simmer until the rice is soft and has absorbed all the water (approximately 15 minutes). Remove from the heat and leave to cool.

Grind the meat in a food processor and add the meat to the cold rice, mixing in well. There should be an equal ratio of rice to meat in the balls. The mixture should be slightly moist but easy to form into small balls. If your mix is too wet, add a little flour or bread crumbs to it.

Form the mix into even size balls. Roll the rice balls in the flour until lightly covered.

Roll in the egg wash and then in the bread crumbs. At this stage the croquettes may be refrigerated and kept until the next day.

Deep-fry in hot oil (365°F), until golden and crispy on the outside. Sprinkle with parsley and serve.

Note: The croquettes may be reheated in a microwave.

Aves

Chicken
Tapas

Chicken in Batter with Honey and Mustard

Pollo Rebozado con Miel y Mostaza

3 chicken breasts, cut into
1-in cubes
Salt and freshly ground
black pepper
2 eggs
Flour, to coat
4 Tbsp olive oil
½ cup honey
1 tsp French mustard
1 tsp soy sauce

preparation

Place the chicken pieces in a bowl. Season. Break the eggs over the chicken pieces and mix in thoroughly, using your hands.

Add enough flour to make a thick coating over the chicken. The egg and flour mixture should be of a consistency where it stops just short of dripping.

Heat the oil in a skillet and fry the chicken until golden, turning frequently, for about 15 minutes.

Remove from the heat, sprinkle with salt and pepper.

Blend the honey with the mustard and soy sauce. Drizzle the honey mixture over the chicken and serve immediately.

Spanish Chicken Pie

Empanada de Pollo

1 lb pastry and topping, as
for recipe for
Spanish Squid Pie (see
page 24)

For the filling
4 Tbsp olive oil
1 onion, chopped
½ lb bacon, chopped
3 tsp garlic, crushed
1 green bell pepper, seeded
and sliced
2 chiles, seeded and
chopped
1 tsp paprika
¾ cup button mushrooms,
sliced
⅔ cup raisins (optional)
2 tsp parsley, chopped
2 tsp soy sauce
⅔ cup dry white wine
1¼ cups chicken broth
¼ stick butter
2 lb chicken meat, boned
and cubed

preparation

Heat the oil. Gently cook the onion and bacon in it.

Add the garlic, bell pepper, chiles, paprika, sliced
mushrooms, and raisins, if using. Stir and add the
parsley and soy sauce. Pour on the wine and broth,
stir, and simmer for 20 minutes.

In a separate pan, melt the butter and add the
chicken cubes. Toss until browned all over and add to
the vegetables. Stir and simmer for 5 minutes.

Remove from heat.

Grease and line a paella pan (dish for 2) with half the
dough. Add the filling; the pie will rise to fill pan.
Cover with slices of tomato and a little salt.

Roll out the remaining dough, sealing the edges well.
Glaze with the egg yolk and decorate as desired.
Leave to stand for 10 minutes before baking.

Bake in the oven at 400°F for 30 minutes. Leave to
cool, and slice to serve.

Note: If you wish to make individual *empanadas,* cut
out 6-inch rounds of pastry. Place the filling in one
half and cover with the remaining dough, sealing well.

Chicken Livers with Sherry Vinegar

Higaditos de Pollo con Vinagre de Jerez

1 lb chicken livers
1 tsp paprika
1 tsp garlic
½ tsp each salt and freshly ground black pepper
½ stick butter, melted
½ onion, chopped fine
¼ cup sherry vinegar
1 tsp sugar
1¼ cups chicken broth
⅓ stick butter

preparation

Wash and trim the chicken livers to remove the green bile sacs and any gristle.

Mix the paprika, garlic, salt, and pepper together in a bowl. Toss the livers to cover in the mix.

Heat the ½ stick of melted butter in a large skillet. Cook the livers over high heat in the butter, stirring continuously, until sealed and browned all over. Place livers in a warmed bowl.

Add the onion to the pan and soften over a lower heat. Turn up the heat again, add the vinegar and sugar, and cook until the vinegar is almost dry. Add the broth, stir, and reduce to half the quantity.

Take the remaining ½ stick butter, break into small pieces, and stir until it melts into the liquid. Check the seasoning and pour the sauce over the livers. Serve in a large bowl or in smaller, individual ones.

Chicken in Garlic Sauce

Pollo al Ajillo

2 lb chicken wings, or
3 chicken breasts
Enough seasoned flour to
coat the chicken pieces
¼ cup olive oil
2 Tbsp butter
½ cup white wine
¼ cup of chicken broth
3 tsp garlic, crushed
1 Tbsp parsley, chopped
Generous Tbsp sherry
Generous Tbsp brandy
Salt and freshly ground
black pepper
Parsley, to garnish

preparation

Cut the chicken into small chunks and toss in the flour until evenly coated.

Heat the oil and butter in a pan. Cook the chicken in the pan until golden, turning quickly to seal all sides.

Add the wine, chicken broth, garlic, and parsley. Simmer to reduce the liquid by half. Stir. Add the sherry and brandy.

Season and serve, garnished with the parsley.

Chicken and Bacon with Mussels

Pollo con Bacon y Mejillones

¼ cup olive oil
1 onion, chopped
6 slices of bacon, cut into strips
3 chicken breasts, cubed and tossed in seasoned flour
⅔ cup dry white wine
2 cups mushrooms, sliced fine
2 tsp garlic, crushed
2½ cups fish or chicken broth
2 lb mussels, cleaned (see tip, page 23)
Salt and freshly ground black pepper
2 Tbsp parsley, chopped

preparation

Heat the oil in a pan. Add the onion and cook gently.

Turn up the heat, add the bacon, and stir. Add the chicken pieces and stir again to seal the meat all over.

In a separate pot, heat the wine, mushrooms, and garlic until reduced by half, then add to the chicken.

Add the chicken or fish broth and bring to a boil.

Add the mussels. Cover the pan with a lid, and shake. Cook until the mussels open. Season well, spoon into hot bowls, and garnish with the parsley.

Meat Tapas

Carnes

Lamb with Apricot Sauce

Cordero con Salsa de Albaricoque

1½ lb lamb fillet

Salt and freshly ground black pepper

Oil or butter, to fry

For the sauce

¼ cup vegetable oil

½ stick butter

1 tsp garlic, crushed

6 oz can apricots, puréed

⅓ cup peanut butter

Juice of 1 lemon, to taste

Salt and freshly ground black pepper

Parsley, to garnish

preparation

Cut the lamb into 1-inch cubes and season. Thread onto skewers and broil, or cook in hot oil or melted butter in a pan until tender, approximately 5 minutes.

to prepare the sauce

Melt the oil and butter together and add the garlic. Whisk in the puréed apricots and the peanut butter.

Do not allow the peanut butter to become too hot; remove from the pan when half-melted.

Add the lemon juice and season to taste. Serve with the lamb pieces. Garnish with parsley.

Marinated Lamb Cutlets

Chuletas de Cordero Marinadas

6 lamb cutlets, trimmed of
excess fat

For the marinade
2 tsp paprika
1 tsp ground cumin
1 tsp turmeric
1 red chile, chopped
1 Tbsp mint, chopped
4 Tbsp olive oil

preparation

Combine all the marinade ingredients and brush liberally over the cutlets.

Marinate in the refrigerator for at least 1 hour.

To cook, bake at 400°F until cooked through (approximately 20 to 25 minutes), or broil, allowing 6 minutes each side. Although these cutlets don't really need a sauce, the following sour cream-based dip complements them well:

> 1 cup sour cream
> 1/3 cup dried apricots, chopped fine
> Freshly ground black pepper

Combine the three ingredients in a bowl or food processor and serve on the side.

Meatballs with Garlic and Tomato

Albondigas con Ajo y Tomate

2 lb lamb, ground
¼ cup bread crumbs
Salt and freshly ground black pepper
2 tsp garlic, crushed
½ tsp nutmeg
2 eggs
¼ cup seasoned flour
¼ cup olive oil
1 large onion, chopped
1 green bell pepper, cut into strips
8 oz can chopped plum tomatoes, or two large tomatoes, skinned and chopped rough
1 Tbsp tomato paste
⅔ cup dry red wine
¾ cup chicken broth
1 Tbsp parsley, chopped

preparation

In a large bowl, mix the lamb with the bread crumbs and season well. Add 1 teaspoon of the crushed garlic, the nutmeg, and the eggs. Form into small meatballs, then roll in the flour.

Heat the oil in a large pan, and cook the onion and bell pepper until tender. Add the meatballs and fry until browned on all sides, stirring well. Add the remaining garlic, tomatoes, tomato paste, wine, and broth. Cover and simmer for 40 minutes.

Season, stir in the parsley, and serve. Add a little sugar if the sauce is too sharp.

Note: These may be prepared in advance and then reheated.

Spanish Smoked Ham

Jamón Serrano

¾ lb jamón serrano,
Smithfield country-cured
ham, prosciutto or
Westphalian ham, finely
sliced and rolled
2½ cups stuffed olives
Lemon wedges, to serve

preparation

Jamón serrano is a smoked ham from Spain. It is usually served sliced thin and is delicious with melon.

Spike cocktail sticks with a roll of ham and an olive, alternately, and serve with lemon wedges.

Spanish Smoked Ham with Tomato and Garlic Toast

Pan con Tomate y Ajo y Jamón Serrano

6 slices of garlic bread (see
Garlic Bread, page 40)
2 large tomatoes, sliced and
dredged with vinaigrette
(see page 45)
½ lb jamón serrano,
Smithfield country-cured
ham, prosciutto, or
Westphalian ham,
sliced fine
1 red onion, sliced fine
½ cup stuffed olives,
chopped

preparation

Prepare the garlic bread and bake in a hot oven until crisp around the edges.

Place a slice of tomato and a slice of ham on the toast, and top with the onion and olives.

This makes an ideal savory finger-food.

Baked Chorizo Sausage

Chorizos Horneados

preparation

This delicious spicy sausage is readily available in a number of grocery and specialty stores.

Slice the sausage into rounds, place in a hot oven (480°F), and bake until just beginning to crisp around the edges, approximately 10 minutes. Serve with plenty of bread.

Chunked Pork in Orange Sauce

Cerdo a la Naranja

½ stick butter or ¼ cup olive oil

1 small onion, sliced fine

1½ lb pork fillet, cut into 1-in cubes

Grated rind of 2 oranges

Juice of 3 oranges

¾ cup chicken broth

2 green chiles, chopped, or 2 tsp chili paste

1 tsp garlic, crushed

1 Tbsp cilantro or parsley, chopped

2 tsp cornstarch

1 Tbsp cold water

Salt and freshly ground black pepper

Parsley, to garnish

preparation

In a large skillet, heat the butter or oil. Sauté the onion until soft and golden, and place aside.

Add the pork to the pan and cook, turning until it is browned on all sides.

Combine the orange rind, orange juice, broth, chile, garlic, and cilantro or parsley together, and pour over the pork. Bring to a boil and add the onion slices. Simmer for 10 minutes. Place in a warm bowl.

Mix the cornstarch and water and add to the sauce to thicken it. Stir, season, and pour over the meat. Garnish with parsley and serve.

Meat and Vegetable Soup

Caldo Gallego

½ stick butter
1 onion, chopped
1 lb bacon or ham
½ tsp garlic, crushed
10 cups broth or water
1½ lb potatoes, peeled and
cut into small chunks
1 small, firm green cabbage,
shredded fine
Freshly ground black pepper
Crusty bread, to serve

preparation

Note: If using pork knuckle, simmer for 1½ hours first.

Melt the butter in a large saucepan. Add the onion and cook gently until soft. Stir in the bacon and garlic.

Pour the broth or water over the garlic and onion, add the potatoes, cover, and cook for 15 minutes. Add the cabbage and cook for a further 5 minutes.

Remove lid, and sprinkle with black pepper. The soup should be thick; if you need to thicken, remove half the greens and potato, and mash before returning to the pan.

Season and serve in bowls, with crusty bread.

Kidneys in Sherry Sauce

Riñones en Salsa de Jerez

1½ lb lamb or veal kidneys
¾ cup olive oil
2 tsp garlic, crushed
1 tsp paprika
2 onions, chopped
½ cup sherry
1¼ cups chicken broth
Salt and freshly ground
black pepper
4 tsp parsley, chopped
3 slices of bread

preparation

Clean the kidneys, removing the hard core and any fat. Slice thinly with a sharp knife.

Bring a pan of water to a boil and plunge the kidneys in for one minute to remove the bitterness.

Heat the oil and fry half the kidneys, with 1 teaspoon of the garlic and ½ teaspoon of the paprika. Cook quickly, stirring so that the garlic does not burn. When cooked, blend in a food processor. Keep to one side.

In the same pan, cook the onions until soft. Place the remaining kidneys in the pan with the other teaspoon of garlic and ½ teaspoon of paprika, and the sherry and broth. Bring to a boil.

Lower the heat, add the puréed kidneys, stir and simmer until the whole kidneys are tender (approximately 5 minutes). Season and serve garnished with chopped parsley, and bread.

Fried Lamb with Lemon Juice

Cordero Frito con Limón

1¾ lb trimmed tender lamb, in strips
Salt and freshly ground black pepper
2 Tbsp olive oil
1 onion, chopped
2 garlic cloves, chopped fine
2 tsp paprika
1 cup broth or water
Juice of 1 lemon
2 Tbsp parsley, chopped fine

preparation

Season the lamb with salt and pepper. Heat the oil in a heatproof casserole over a very high heat and add the meat in handfuls. Add the onion and a little garlic, and keep turning the meat with a wooden spoon. Add more meat and garlic as each batch seals, with more oil if necessary.

When the meat is golden and the onion is soft, sprinkle with paprika and add the broth or water. Continue cooking over a medium heat until the liquid is almost dry.

Sprinkle with the lemon juice and parsley, cover and simmer for 5 minutes. Season to taste and serve.

Small Spicy Moorish Kabobs

Pinchitos Morunos

2 garlic cloves, chopped fine

2 tsp salt

1 tsp mild curry powder

1/2 tsp coriander seeds

1 tsp paprika

1/4 tsp dried thyme

Freshly ground black pepper

3 Tbsp olive oil

1 Tbsp lemon juice

Lime wedges, to serve

1 lb lean pork, cut into small cubes

preparation

Crush the chopped garlic with the salt using a pestle and mortar (or the flat of a knife on a board).

Work the curry powder, coriander seeds, paprika, thyme, black pepper, olive oil, and lemon juice into the garlic and salt. Set the marinade aside in a shallow dish.

Remove any excess fat from the pork and chop into small bite-size cubes. Skewer the meat, 3 to 4 cubes to a small stick, and turn the kabobs in the shallow dish to coat thoroughly with the marinade. Leave to marinate for at least a couple of hours. The longer you leave them, the better the flavor.

Arrange the kabobs, spreading them well apart, on aluminum foil under the broiler, or on a barbecue. Cook under (or over) a high heat until the meat is browned on the outside and cooked through. This should take about 3 minutes on each side.

Serve immediately with lime wedges.

Note: Europe's first kabobs were brought by the Arabs from North Africa. They are eaten everywhere in Spain as a *tapa*, though nowadays they are made from pork, rather than the original lamb. Spices for them are sold ready-mixed in southern Spain. The curry powder used in this recipe contains cumin and other identical herbs to those used in Spain.